GIANT PANDAS ARE AWESOME

by Samantha S. Bell

12 STORY LIBRARY

www.12StoryLibrary.com

12-Story Library is an imprint of Bookstaves and Press Room Editions

Produced for 12-Story Library by Red Line Editorial

Photographs ©: leungchopan/Shutterstock Images, cover, 1; Hung Chung Chih/Shutterstock Images, 4, 10, 11, 15, 19, 21, 26, 29; Yusei/Shutterstock Images, 5; Volodymyr Goinyk/Shutterstock Images, 6, 12; dangdumrong/Shutterstock Images, 7; SJ Travel Photo and Video/Shutterstock Images, 8; tomava/Shutterstock Images, 9, 28; russal/Shutterstock Images, 13; Dennis W Donohue/Shutterstock Images, 14; Olga Kot Photo/Shutterstock Images, 16; Birdiegal/Shutterstock Images, 17; Don Mammoser/Shutterstock Images, 18; Orhan Cam/Shutterstock Images, 20, 25; Alexandra Giese/Shutterstock Images, 22; plavevski/Shutterstock Images, 23, 24, 27

Library of Congress Cataloging-in-Publication Data
Names: Bell, Samantha, author.
Title: Giant pandas are awesome / by Samantha Bell.
Description: Mankato, MN : 12 Story Library, 2017. | Series: Animals are awesome | Includes bibliographical references and index. | Audience: Grades 4 to 6.
Identifiers: LCCN 2016047098 (print) | LCCN 2017005249 (ebook) | ISBN 9781632354358 (hardcover : alk. paper) | ISBN 9781632355034 (pbk. : alk. paper) | ISBN 9781621435556 (hosted e-book)
Subjects: LCSH: Giant panda--Juvenile literature.
Classification: LCC QL737.C27 B438 2017 (print) | LCC QL737.C27 (ebook) | DDC 599.789--dc23
LC record available at https://lccn.loc.gov/2016047098

Printed in China
022017

Table of Contents

Pandas Can Grow as Tall as Humans 4

Pandas Are Shy 6

Pandas Spend Half the Day Eating 8

Pandas Have Fake Thumbs 10

Pandas Do Not Hibernate 12

Pandas Are Great Tree Climbers 14

Pandas Are Loners 16

Pandas Chirp, Bleat, and Honk 18

Male Pandas Take Dust Baths 20

Baby Pandas Are Very Tiny 22

Mother Pandas Hold Their New Babies 24

Giant Pandas Are No Longer Endangered 26

Fact Sheet 28

Glossary 30

For More Information 31

Index 32

About the Author 32

1

Pandas Can Grow as Tall as Humans

For many years, scientists wondered what type of animal giant pandas were. They did not know if pandas belonged to the bear or raccoon family or if they were a species all their own. By studying their DNA cells, scientists discovered giant pandas are true bears.

Like other bears, giant pandas have stocky bodies and short tails. They have teeth for tearing meat. Their stomachs have enzymes for digesting the meat. Giant pandas are

Pandas are some of the most shy animals on Earth.

THE WORLD WILDLIFE FUND LOGO

The World Wildlife Fund (WWF) works to preserve wildlife and the environment. It was created in 1961. That same year, a giant panda named Chi-Chi arrived at the London Zoo. She was beautiful, endangered, and well loved. The founders of the WWF knew she would make a perfect logo for their organization.

also similar to other bears in how they climb.

But giant panda bears are unusual. Almost all of their diet is made up of plants. They have flat teeth for grinding their food. When they eat, they hold on to their food the same way a raccoon does. They do not roar like other bears.

Giant pandas stand approximately four to five feet (1.2 to 1.5 m) tall, about the same height as an American black bear. Males can weigh up to 300 pounds (136 kg). Females are smaller. Giant pandas are well known for their black-and-white markings, and their coats are thick and woolly. With their teddy bear–like features, giant pandas are loved by people around the world.

220

Number of pounds (100 kg) a female giant panda can weigh.

- Giant pandas are true bears.
- Pandas have a woolly black-and-white coat.
- Pandas have flat teeth for grinding plants.
- Grown pandas are about the size of an American black bear.

2

Pandas Are Shy

At one time, giant pandas lived throughout southern and eastern China, Myanmar, and northern Vietnam. But pandas are shy and avoid people. They will not wander into areas where people live. When humans started moving into the pandas' habitat, the bears moved away. Now, pandas are only found in six mountain ranges in China's Sichuan, Shaanxi, and Gansu provinces.

Giant pandas live in coniferous forests with at least two kinds of bamboo. Every 20 to 40 years, bamboo plants flower and die. It can take four years or more to grow again. Other bamboo needs to be available.

Pandas live in remote parts of China, far from humans.

67

Number of nature reserves in China for pandas.

- Giant pandas live only in remote mountain regions in China.
- Giant pandas do not venture into places where people are.
- Pandas need coniferous forests with at least two bamboo species.

A giant panda in a tree in Chengdu, China

A NATIONAL TREASURE

Pandas are considered a national treasure in China. They are a symbol of the history and culture of the Chinese people. Pandas are even found in Chinese art created thousands of years ago.

The forests where giant pandas live are cool and wet. There is often pouring rain, a thick mist, or heavy clouds. Most pandas make their homes at elevations of 5,000 to 10,000 feet (1,500 to 3,000 m). In the summer, they may go as high as 13,000 feet (4,000 m).

To protect the giant panda's remaining habitat, China has created nature reserves. Two-thirds of wild pandas live in these nature reserves. The rest of the pandas roam in areas close by.

3

Pandas Spend Half the Day Eating

Giant pandas are omnivores, eating both plants and meat. Sometimes, they eat birds and rodents. But mostly they eat bamboo. Bamboo stems, leaves, and young shoots make up 99 percent of a giant panda's diet.

Bamboo is a plant that is very low in nutrients, so giant pandas need a lot of it. Adult pandas eat about 28 pounds (13 kg) of bamboo every day. They spend 12 to 14 hours a day eating.

The digestive system of a giant panda is like that of other bears. It contains microbes for digesting meat, not plants. So when pandas eat bamboo,

Pandas are classified as meat-eaters, but they mainly eat bamboo.

THINK ABOUT IT

A giant panda's typical day includes a lot of eating and napping and a little playing. How does this compare with the typical day of other kinds of bears?

Pandas digest approximately a fifth of the food they eat.

most of it cannot be used by their bodies. Giant pandas can digest about only 17 percent of the bamboo they eat. Because the bamboo does not provide much energy, giant pandas are not very active. After each feeding, a giant panda will nap for two to four hours.

20

Number of species of bamboo giant pandas will eat.

- Pandas are omnivores.
- A panda's diet is 99 percent bamboo.
- Pandas eat 28 pounds (13 kg) of bamboo a day.
- Giant pandas will eat birds and rodents.

4

Pandas Have Fake Thumbs

When giant pandas eat, they often sit on the ground with their hind legs stretched out in front of them. They have an extra digit on their front paws that helps them hold, turn, and handle the bamboo. Scientists call this digit a "pseudo-thumb," but it is not really a thumb. It is a special bone that extends from the wrist.

Pandas have unusual teeth. Their molars and premolars are wider and flatter than those of other bears. They use these teeth to grind bamboo. With their strong jawbones and cheek muscles, they can crush bamboo stalks up to 1.5 inches (3.8 cm) in diameter.

Even though the giant panda's body

Pandas use their pseudo-thumbs to help them rip apart bamboo.

Pandas have large molars for eating bamboo.

cannot use most of the bamboo it eats, its digestive system can process it. The panda's esophagus has a thick lining that protects it from splinters. Its stomach is protected by a thick layer of mucus. The stomach walls are extra muscular, which helps the panda digest the woody part of the bamboo.

6

Number of digits a giant panda has on each of its front paws.

- Pandas use their pseudo-thumbs to hold bamboo.
- Giant pandas have strong jawbones, cheek muscles, and flat back teeth to chew thick bamboo stalks.
- The lining in a panda's digestive system protects it from bamboo splinters.

USING PANDA POOP

With so much undigested bamboo, it is no wonder giant pandas create a lot of waste. One panda can make about 88 pounds (40 kg) of waste a day. People are finding uses for panda waste. It is used to make paper and souvenirs. One man is using it to make tea. Scientists are trying to find a way to use it as fuel.

5

Pandas Do Not Hibernate

Giant pandas need habitats with large, old trees. The trees provide shelter and nutrients for the bamboo pandas eat. They also provide hollow logs and stumps that are big enough for the pandas to use as dens. The pandas use the dens to raise their cubs. But they do not use them to hibernate. Giant pandas stay active all winter long.

The pandas' bamboo diet does not allow them to store enough fat for the winter. Giant pandas cannot rest when the weather turns cold. They have to keep eating. But unlike other bears, pandas can find their main food source all year round.

Pandas take shelter in caves and hollow trees when the weather is very cold.

The cold of winter can freeze the mountain streams where pandas get their water. So the pandas move down the mountains to an elevation of approximately 5,000 feet (1,500 m). There, they can find flowing water and more bamboo to eat.

68

Temperature, in degrees Fahrenheit (20°C), some giant pandas prefer.

- Pandas use hollow logs and tree stumps for dens.
- Pandas eat bamboo all year round.
- Pandas do not have enough fat to hibernate.
- In the winter, pandas climb down to a lower elevation.

THINK ABOUT IT

Giant pandas in captivity love to play in the snow. With the help of a teacher or parent, find some videos online of pandas in the snow. Do you think pandas in the wild react the same way?

Pandas get a lot of water from bamboo, but they also need a supply of fresh drinking water.

6 Pandas Are Great Tree Climbers

Because pandas do not get much energy from the bamboo they eat, they are usually slow moving. But when facing a predator, a panda can act quickly. Healthy adult pandas are not threatened by other animals. But young, small, or weak pandas may be attacked by leopards, brown bears, wolves, or jackals.

To escape a predator, pandas sometimes hide in the thick forest. The pattern of their black-and-white

The snow leopard is a predator of giant pandas.

fur helps camouflage them. They are almost invisible in the thick patches of bamboo.

Pandas can climb trees quickly and easily to get away from predators.

Pandas are good at climbing trees. Their claws and furry undersides help them grip the trunk. The trees are a safe place to be. When threatened, young pandas race to the nearest tree. Small bears can climb higher than predators. Cubs climb trees to wait for their mothers.

110

Number of pounds (50 kg) a young panda must weigh to be safe from predators.

- Pandas climb trees to escape predators.
- Pandas are threatened by jackals, leopards, brown bears, and wolves.
- A giant panda's claws and furry underside help it grip trees.

7

Pandas Are Loners

Most giant pandas prefer to live alone in their own territory. But the territories of male pandas often overlap, and pandas sometimes cross paths. They may growl or swat at each other. They might bob their heads up and down. Sometimes, pandas lunge at each other. But mostly, they try to avoid contact. The smaller panda will give in to the larger panda by tucking its head between its legs or covering its eyes.

To mark its territory, a giant panda uses a large scent gland near its tail. Both male and female pandas leave scent marks. Each bear's

Pandas prefer to live alone and will sometimes fight with one another if they meet up.

scent is unique. Pandas rub their scents on trees, rocks, stumps, logs, and the ground. Then, they use their tails like brushes to spread it around.

Giant pandas have a strong sense of smell. When a panda finds a scent mark, it can figure out the gender, age, and even identity of the bear that left the mark. It can also tell how long the scent has been there. Pandas use this information to communicate with each other.

1.9

Number of square miles (4.9 sq. km) in a giant panda's territory.

- Pandas prefer to live alone.
- If two pandas cross paths, they'll growl, swat, and lunge at each other.
- Both male and female pandas leave scent marks.
- Each panda's scent is unique.

8

Pandas Chirp, Bleat, and Honk

Some animals use body language to communicate. They may point their ears forward when they are curious or flatten them to show fright. They may use their tails as a signal. Or their fur might stand up when they are angry. But giant pandas do not communicate in any of these ways. Their ears are not flexible, and their tails are too short.

Instead, giant pandas use a lot of different sounds to communicate. They honk, huff, bark, and growl. Sometimes, pandas bleat a friendly greeting. They make a noise that sounds similar to one a lamb or baby goat makes. Other times, pandas bark like a dog.

Pandas communicate with one another fairly often.

13

Number of different sounds giant pandas make.

- Giant pandas do not use body language.
- Pandas make the most sounds of all the bear species.
- They use many different sounds to communicate.
- Pandas are most vocal during mating season.

Pandas make different sounds if they are playful, hungry, or frightened.

Young panda cubs squeal or croak. Giant pandas are the most vocal of all the bear species.

Pandas make the most noise during mating season. Loud moans from a female means she is looking for a mate. The moans can sound like a low moo, a whine, or even a hoot. Males use sounds such as chomping, clicking, and smacking to get a female's attention.

9

Male Pandas Take Dust Baths

The giant panda's strong sense of smell keeps it away from other pandas most of the year. But during mating season, that sense of smell helps bring male and female pandas together. Mating season for giant pandas is from March through May. During this time, males are attracted to the scents of females who are ready to mate.

Female pandas are more likely to mate with a male whose scent she has smelled before.

Males often claw the bark on tree trunks. This helps leave behind their scent to attract females. Sometimes the males roll around in the dust. The dust particles become covered with the panda's scent and drift through the air.

Pandas remain alone most of the year. They come together during mating season.

5

Number of male giant pandas that may compete over a female.

- Giant pandas start mating when they are five to seven years old.
- Mating season runs from March to May.
- The pandas' sense of smell helps males and females find each other.
- Several males will compete to mate with a female.

Male pandas start looking for a mate when they are about seven years old. Females need to be five to six years old. When the female is ready, several males will come to her. The male pandas may fight over the female by pushing, swatting, lunging at, or wrestling with each other. They may try to bite each other on the neck or shoulders.

10

Baby Pandas Are Very Tiny

The female giant panda mates only in the spring. After mating, the male panda moves on. He does not help raise the cub. The female eats 20 hours a day to give the unborn cub as many nutrients as possible.

In late summer, most often in August, the mother panda will choose a hollow tree or a cave for a den. She lines it with bamboo twigs. The female gives birth between 95 and 160 days after mating. She may have one or two cubs, but usually only one survives.

The newborn panda is a pinkish-white color. It is blind and helpless. The newborn is approximately six inches (15 cm) long, 900 times

Male and female pandas do not stay together after they mate.

5

Number of cubs a female giant panda may raise in her lifetime.

- Baby pandas are born 95 to 160 days after the mother and father mate.
- Females may have two cubs, but in most cases, only one survives.
- Giant pandas are helpless when they are born.

Baby pandas are the size of a stick of butter.

smaller than the size of its mother. It weighs just three to five ounces (85 to 142 g). The mother panda carefully tends to her tiny cub. She will stay in the den for several days after birth. She will not leave even to eat or drink.

HEY, YOU!

All pandas belong to China. China loans them to zoos in other countries, so any cubs the pandas have are on loan, too. In China, tradition says children must wait 100 days to receive their names to keep bad luck away. Zoos also often wait 100 days to name newborn cubs.

11

Mother Pandas Hold Their New Babies

A mother panda will sit with her back to the den opening to keep her cub warm. She holds her new baby with her front paws most of the time for the first few weeks. The baby panda nurses up to 14 times a day. It needs its mother's milk for at least eight to nine months, drinking less as it gets older.

At about one to three weeks old, the cub starts to get its black-and-white coloring. Its eyes open when it is seven to eight weeks old. At 12 weeks, the cub can finally crawl. Just a month later, the mother and cub start leaving the den area together. The cub plays by

Newborn pandas can barely move on their own for their first three months.

Mother pandas are very protective of their cubs.

rolling around on the ground and climbing on its mother.

By the time the cub is about five months old, it is moving better. It is still unsteady, but it can walk fairly well. At approximately seven to nine months, the cub begins eating bamboo. Still, it will often continue to nurse. The cub stops nursing when it is about a year and a half old. By that time, the cub is old enough to find its own territory. When the cub leaves, its mother gets ready to find another mate.

6

Age, in months, of a cub when it starts climbing trees.

- Cubs are blind until they are two months old.
- By five months old, a panda cub can walk and play.
- Cubs start eating bamboo at about nine months old.
- A cub will stay with its mother for about 18 months.

THINK ABOUT IT

When a giant panda in a zoo has two cubs, the zookeepers often help take care of the smaller one. Do you think this is a difficult job? Why or why not?

12 Giant Pandas Are No Longer Endangered

Although grown giant pandas do not have to worry about predators, other things have threatened their survival. For many years, giant pandas were hunted for their fur. People paid a lot of money for a panda's pelt. It was comfortable to wear. And some people believed panda fur had magical powers. Another major threat to pandas was the loss of their habitat as people moved in. Tourists, loggers, and farmers pushed pandas into smaller and smaller areas. By the late 1970s, there were only about 1,000 pandas left in nature.

To help giant pandas rebuild their population, the Chinese government passed many laws against hunting them. It set up nature reserves to protect the pandas' habitat and make it much larger. Zoos began

Many pandas live in zoos throughout the world.

A baby panda born as part of a zoo program

BACK TO NATURE

At the Hetaoping panda center in China, keepers raised panda cubs to be released into nature. They did not want these cubs to become too comfortable around people. To avoid this problem, the keepers wore scented panda costumes when training the cubs.

breeding pandas. In 1990, the giant panda was put on the endangered species list.

38

Number of panda cubs born in captivity in China in 2015.

- Giant pandas were threatened by hunters.
- They were also threatened by habitat destruction.
- China passed many laws to protect giant pandas.
- Giant pandas are no longer on the endangered species list.

Decades later, the panda population has grown. By 2003, there were 1,600 giant pandas in nature. In 2014, scientists counted more than 1,850. Though there are still very few giant pandas in the world, they are making a comeback. They are no longer considered an endangered species.

Fact Sheet

- Giant pandas are not afraid of the water. In fact, they are good swimmers.
- Researchers have found that some pandas live in communities of 7 to 15 bears.
- Pandas will sleep almost anywhere. They may sleep in trees, on the grass, or on rocks.
- Like cats, giant pandas' pupils are slits. This helps them see better at night.
- If a panda feels threatened, it can become violent. Mother pandas are very protective of their cubs.
- Pandas are always eating, even at night. They are the fastest-growing mammals in size.

- Giant pandas live approximately 20 years in the wild. They live approximately 30 years in captivity.
- Pandas climb trees to play. They also climb them to sunbathe or take a nap.

Glossary

coniferous
Made up of evergreen trees and shrubs.

elevation
The height above sea level.

hibernate
To sleep or rest through the winter.

jackals
Wild dogs in Asia or Africa that are smaller than wolves.

microbes
Organisms that are microscopic in size.

molars
Teeth with a round or flattened surface for grinding.

mucus
A sticky, slippery substance that moistens and protects.

nutrients
Things that provide nourishment and cause growth.

pelt
The skin and fur of an animal.

predator
An animal that lives by hunting, killing, and eating other animals.

rodents
Small mammals that have sharp front teeth for gnawing, such as squirrels or mice.

For More Information

Books

Angel, Heather. *Panda: An Intimate Portrait of One of the World's Most Elusive Characters*. Exeter, UK: David and Charles, 2008.

Jazynka, Kitson. *Mission: Panda Rescue*. Washington, DC: National Geographic, 2016.

Ryder, Joanne. *Panda Kindergarten*. New York: HarperCollins, 2009.

Index

babies, 18, 24
bamboo, 6, 8, 10–11, 12–13, 14–15, 22, 25
bear, 4–6, 8, 10, 12, 14–15, 16–17, 19
body, 4, 9, 11, 18

China, 6–7
claws, 15, 20
climbing, 5, 15, 25
communicate, 17, 18
cubs, 12, 15, 19, 22–23, 24–25

dens, 12, 22–23, 24

eating, 5, 8–9, 10–11, 12–13, 14, 22–23, 25

females, 5, 16, 19, 20–21, 22
fight, 21

laws, 26

males, 5, 16, 19, 20–21, 22
mate, 19, 20–21, 22, 25
mothers, 15 22–23, 24–25

napping, 9

predators, 14–15, 26
pseudo-thumb, 10

scent, 16–17, 20
smell, 17, 20
stomach, 4, 11

teeth, 4–5, 10
territory, 16, 25
trees, 12, 15, 17, 20, 22

water, 13

About the Author

Samantha S. Bell lives with her family and lots of pets in the foothills of South Carolina. She loves writing about nature, and she is the author or illustrator of more than 60 books for children.